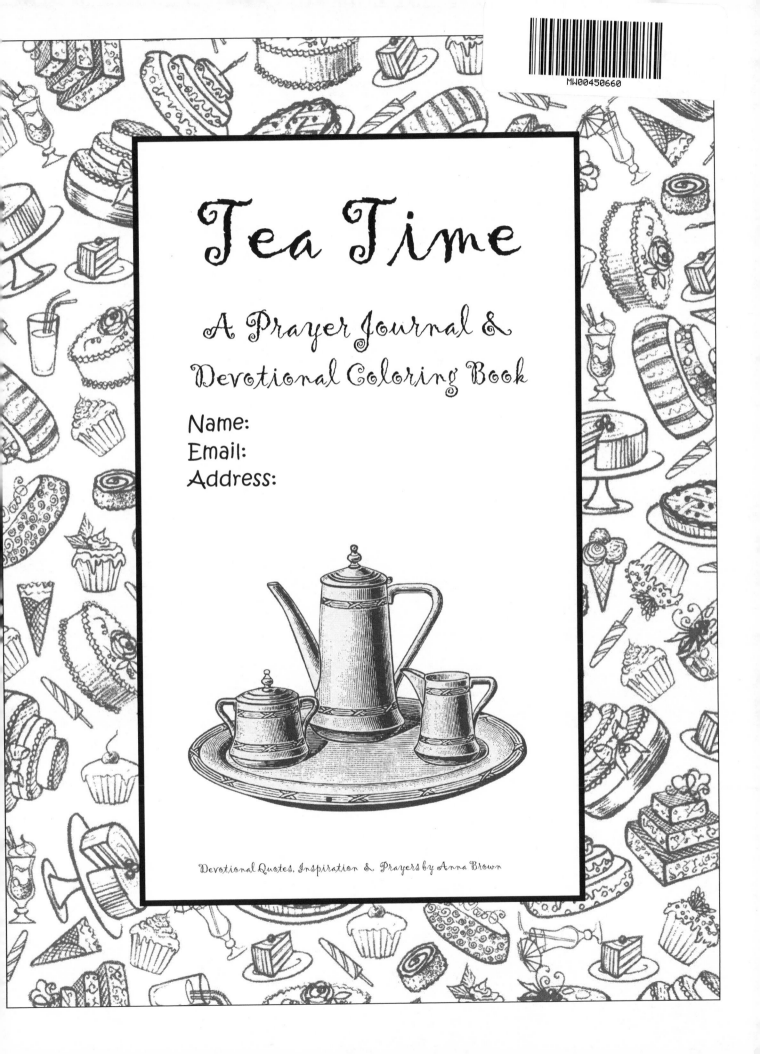

Tea Time

A Prayer Journal &
Devotional Coloring Book

Name:
Email:
Address:

Devotional Quotes, Inspiration & Prayers by Anna Brown

Tea Time Devotional

Time With God

PRAY

Draw

Read

Relax

Hope

Love

Trust

Dream

Make a Tea-Time Basket

Everything you need for Tea-Time should be in a pretty basket.
Spend a little time everyday with your basket of good things!

Fill Your Basket with Good Things!

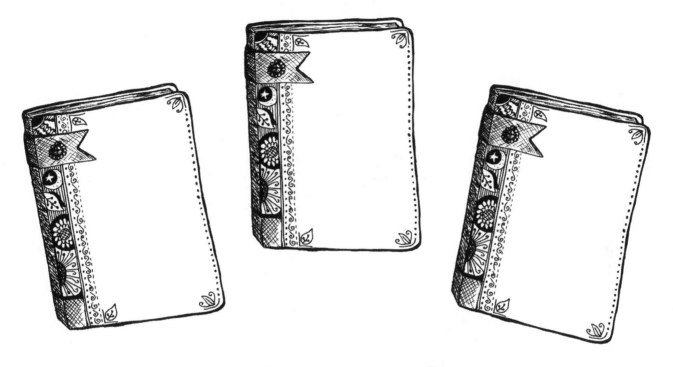

Your Bible, Favorite Books,
This Book, A Smooth Black Pen,
Colored Pencils, Gel Pens, Tea Cup,
Candles, Matches, Tea, Sugar and Cream.

Do You Love to Read?

Take some time out from the digital world and
rediscover the joy of a
good old-fashion paperback book!
Nothing like a good book and a cup of tea!

All The Books you Hope to Read Soon:

Draw the covers of any other books you are
planning to read in the near future. Put them in your basket when
you are ready for a new book.

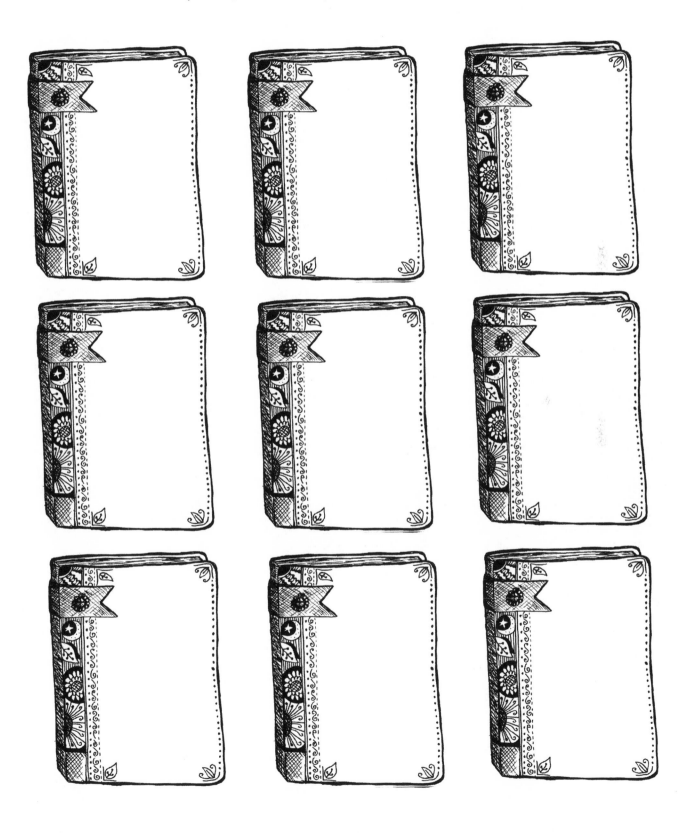

What is on Your Mind?

Draw or write about all the things that have been on your mind lately.
Writing down your thoughts can help you to clear your mind.
Focus on your true priorities and pray for each thought.

"Remember when you feel unloved, unappreciated and
insecure remember Whom you belong to."

The Desires of my Heart..

God will meet us as we seek Him.

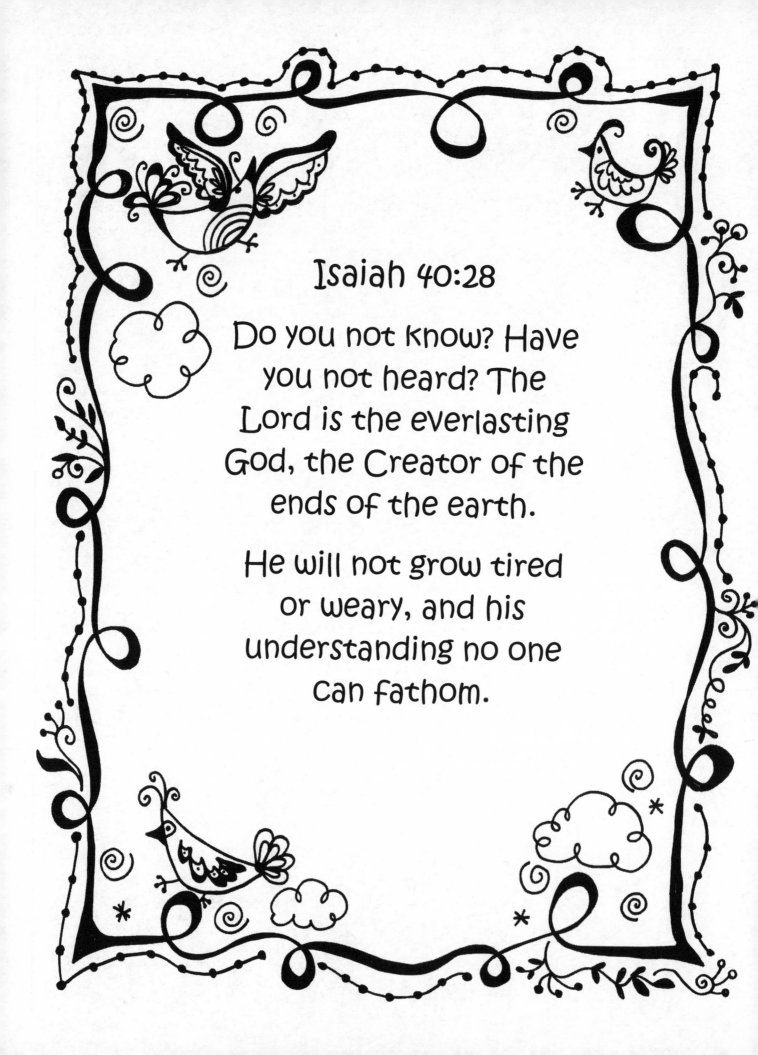

Isaiah 40:28

Do you not know? Have you not heard? The Lord is the everlasting God, the Creator of the ends of the earth.

He will not grow tired or weary, and his understanding no one can fathom.

A Prayer for Love..

Bible Time

Date: _____

Bible Passage: _____

Write a poem...

My Day

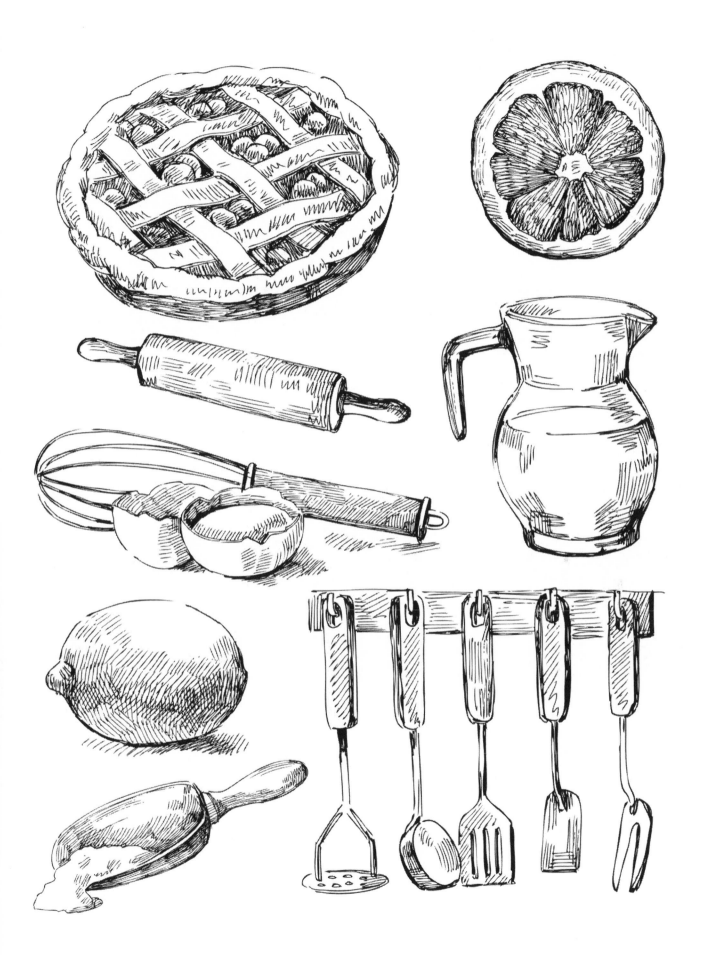

My Thoughts

Draw or write about all the things that have been on your mind lately.
Writing down your thoughts can help you to clear your mind.
Focus on your true priorities and pray for each thought.

"The pain you are feeling
can't compare to the joy that's coming."

Everything...

Everything I am
I give to you, The bad
and the good. Shape
me, come be with me. I
give you my all. It's not
much, My ugly sin
messed up your
beautiful handy work.
Your art I ruined. So I
give myself back to you,
And little by little you
can make me beautiful
again.

Isaiah 9:6

For to us a Child is born, to us a Son is given, and the government will be on His shoulders. And He will be called Wonderful Counselor, Mighty God, Everlasting Father, Prince of Peace.

A Prayer for Joy..

Bible Time

Date:_____

Bible Passage:_____

An Answered Prayer...

I want to be...

Prayers...

Draw or write about all the things that have been on your mind lately.
Writing down your thoughts can help you to clear your mind.
Focus on your true priorities and pray for each thought.

"God sometimes takes us into troubled waters,
Not to drown us, But to cleanse us."

What Do You Want To Be Known For?

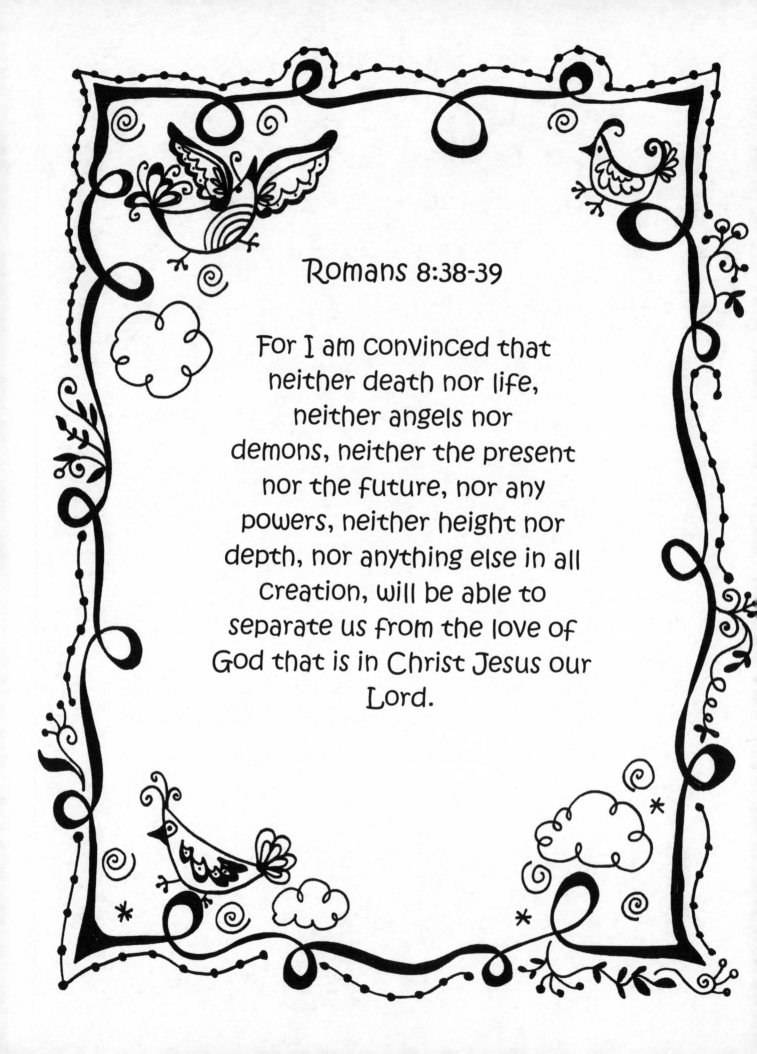

Romans 8:38-39

For I am convinced that neither death nor life, neither angels nor demons, neither the present nor the future, nor any powers, neither height nor depth, nor anything else in all creation, will be able to separate us from the love of God that is in Christ Jesus our Lord.

A Prayer for Peace..

   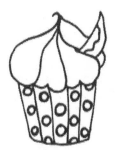

Bible Time

Date: _____

Bible Passage: _____

I'm thankful for..

A Favorite Praise Song

What is on Your Mind?

Draw or write about all the things that have been on your mind lately.
Writing down your thoughts can help you to clear your mind.
Focus on your true priorities and pray for each thought.

"Sometimes God says "Wait. I have a better plan."

Don't Forget...

Jesus payed it all,
and He asks for nothing
in return but your heart.

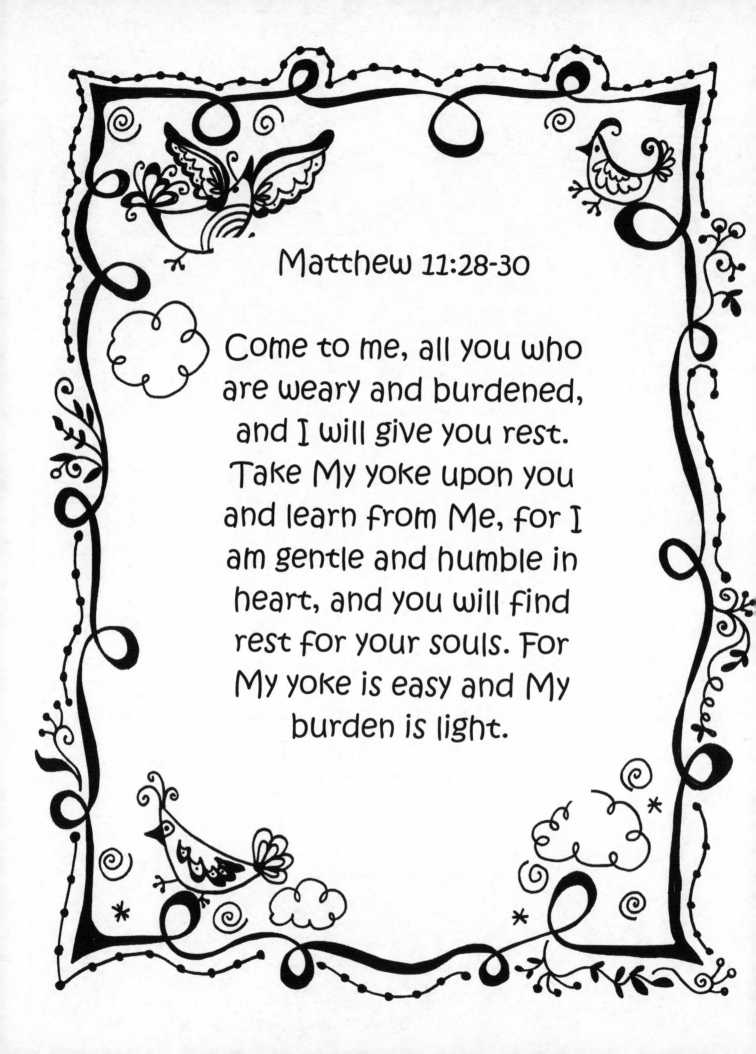

Matthew 11:28-30

Come to me, all you who
are weary and burdened,
and I will give you rest.
Take My yoke upon you
and learn from Me, for I
am gentle and humble in
heart, and you will find
rest for your souls. For
My yoke is easy and My
burden is light.

A Prayer for Patience..

✗ Please give me patience w/ R and his way of dealing with the children.

✗ Please give me patience w/ E and things that come up w/ her personality and how she interacts w/ the boys.

Bible Time

Date:_____

Bible Passage:_____

Change the world.

Make A list of things you can do
to make someone's day.
(And then do them!)

I'm Sorry God for...

Clear your mind.

Draw or write about all the things that have been on your mind lately.
Writing down your thoughts can help you to clear your mind.
Focus on your true priorities and pray for each thought.

*"When a train goes though a tunnel it gets dark, But you
don't throw away your ticket and jump off the train, you
sit still and trust the engineer."*

Grace

Grace is the only reason
I am saved, Jesus gave me grace,
He took the blame for every sin
I have made or ever will make.
I can't be enough, But Jesus can be.

Hebrews 12:1-2

Therefore, since we are
surrounded by such a great
cloud of witnesses, let us
throw off everything that
hinders and the sin that so
easily entangles, and let us
run with perseverance the
race marked out for us.

Let us fix our eyes on Jesus,
the author and perfecter of
our faith, who for the joy set
before Him endured the
cross, scorning its shame,
and sat down at the right
hand of the throne of God.

A Prayer for Strength..

Bible Time

Date:_____

Bible Passage:_____

The Promise

We have a commandment from God. This commandment is for everyone, even for you.

Jesus told his disciples to wait for "the Promise of the Father." The Holy Spirit. If you have received Jesus than pray for the Holy Spirit to influence all your actions, Ask Him to use you in the most effective way possible for your life.

Life on earth is like one tiny grain of sand on a beach that never ends, one breath of air. Heaven is like billions and millions of miles of atmosphere, Life on earth is like one page in a book series the author is still writing. Life on earth is short! We Christians shouldn't waste time, sitting around, watching TV and seeking comfort. We are all about "The Easy Way." Jesus didn't take the easy way to save us from eternal fire. He, God, came from paradise to our messed up world, and not only died but carried the guilt and blame of every sin we ever made or ever will. His Father couldn't even look at him. And we take that gift for granted. Like an orphan that just got adopted. We should be so excited we wanna tell everyone. we should, but we are too busy watching our favorite TV show. That is pathetic.

We have a chance to be part of changing someone's eternal destination, but we are too busy. Plus that might be awkward, It could be unCOMFORTable. First of all, we, Christ followers have a mission. A command!

"But you shall receive power when the Holy Spirit has come upon you, and you shall be witnesses to me in Jerusalem, in all Judea and Samaria and to the ends of the earth." That is God's command to us! We are His disciples! But you will not do this alone and on your own strength, "You will receive power." God will give you strength and power, He will use you to fulfill His mission If you let him. He doesn't want ANYONE to perish. He wants to use you to bring people to Him. He can do amazing things through and in your life, but don't be afraid, He will give you courage and strength and most important He will be with you. So stand up and tell God "Here I am, Use me." and watch Him do it.

Receive God's Promise

What is on Your Mind?

Draw or write about all the things that have been on your mind lately.
Writing down your thoughts can help you to clear your mind.
Focus on your true priorities and pray for each thought.

"I am amazed at what God can do if you say "Here I am, use me!"

Dear God..

You are beautiful!
Make me like You.
I cannot change on my own,
I need Your help. I need
You! Come be with me,
Show me Your unfailing love
again. Be my Father, My
friend and my savior.

God, This prayer goes to
You. In Jesus name, Do far
more than my expectations,
Amen.

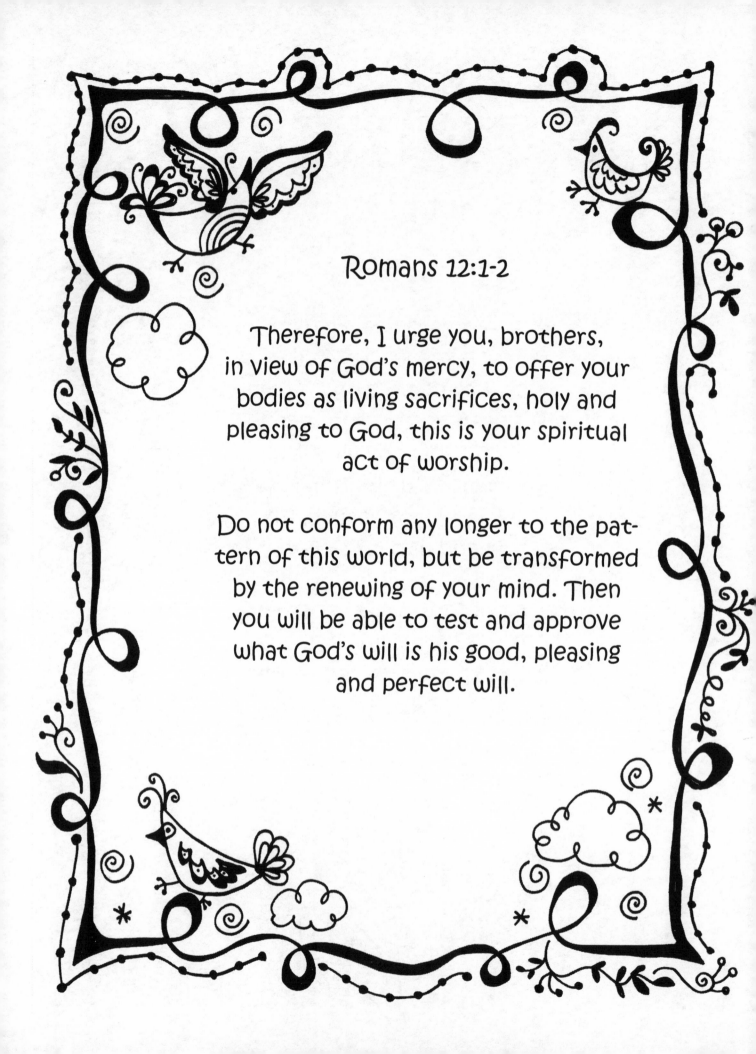

Romans 12:1-2

Therefore, I urge you, brothers, in view of God's mercy, to offer your bodies as living sacrifices, holy and pleasing to God, this is your spiritual act of worship.

Do not conform any longer to the pattern of this world, but be transformed by the renewing of your mind. Then you will be able to test and approve what God's will is his good, pleasing and perfect will.

A Prayer for Faithfulness...

Bible Time

Date:_____

Bible Passage:_____

A Prayer for a Friend in Need...

Hope & Dreams

What is on Your Mind?

Draw or write about all the things that have been on your mind lately.
Writing down your thoughts can help you to clear your mind.
Focus on your true priorities and pray for each thought.

When something goes wrong in your life just yell "Plot twist!" And move on.

Trusting God

Ask God to show Himself to you and be real in your life. We have to give our brokenness to Him and ask Him to save us. We cannot be good enough. We are saved only by His mercy and work on the cross. Salvation is a gift. It's not something we can work for. We can only trust Jesus to be our bridge to the Father.

Trusting God means that even though you have doubts you are choosing to believe in Him and seek Him. He will show his unfailing love to you. He started A good work and He WILL be faithful to complete it.

Psalm 139 1-6

You have searched me, Lord,
and You know me.
You know when I sit and when I rise;
You perceive my thoughts from afar.

You discern my going out and my lying down;
You are familiar with all my ways.

Before a word is on my tongue
You, Lord, know it completely.
You hem me in behind and before,
and you lay Your hand upon me.
Such knowledge is too wonderful for
me, too lofty for me to attain.

A Prayer for Gentleness..

Bible Time

Date: _____

Bible Passage: _____

Write a Poem to God..

My Home...

My Thoughts

Draw or write about all the things that have been on your mind lately.
Writing down your thoughts can help you to clear your mind.
Focus on your true priorities and pray for each thought.

"Prayer should be our first response not our last resort."

Praise God at All Times

I praise You for the night.
I praise You for the storm.
I praise You for the rain. I praise
You for the waves. I praise You for
the darkness. Because now that
it's morning... the storm calmed,
The rain stopped, the waves
flattened, and the darkness
disappeared,

The sunlight is more beautiful
than I ever remembered. I had to
hold Your hand to stay safe and
now I am closer to You than ever
before and now that the darkness
is gone I can see Your face more
clearly than I ever thought I could.

Write a
Favorite Verse

A Prayer for Self Control..

Bible Time

Date: _____

Bible Passage: _____

My Day..

My Favorite Worship Song

What is on Your Mind?

Draw or write about all the things that have been on your mind lately.
Writing down your thoughts can help you to clear your mind.
Focus on your true priorities and pray for each thought.

"When you go through deep waters I will be with you."

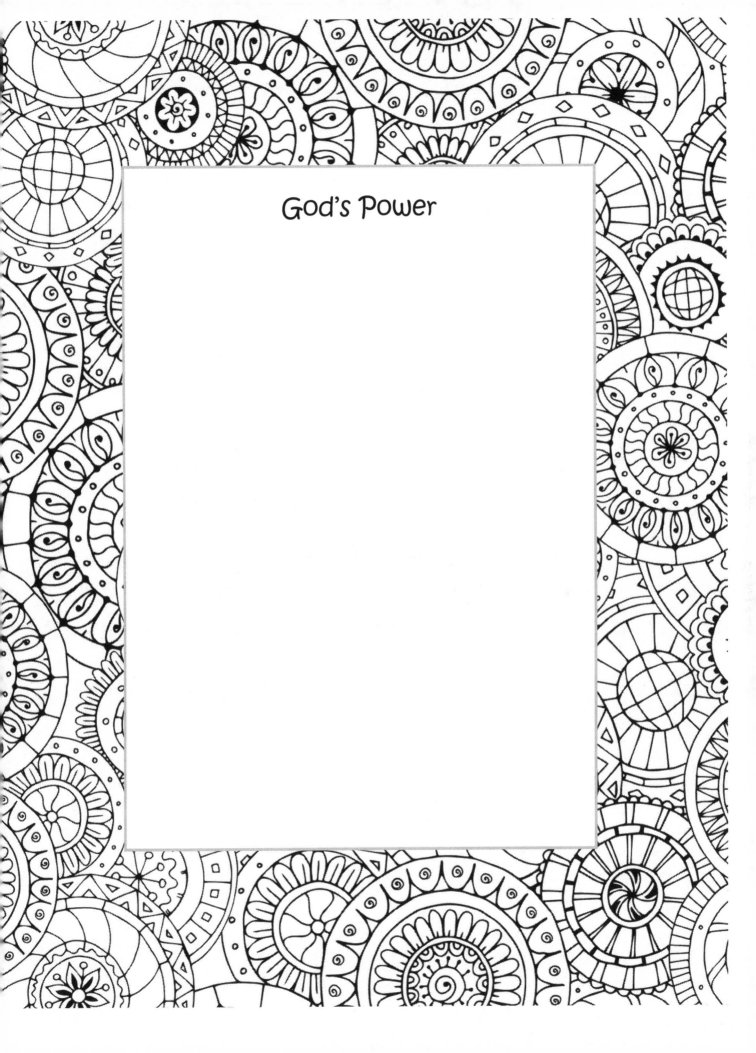

God's Power

Isaiah 40:28

Do you not know? Have you not heard?

The Lord is the everlasting God, the Creator of the ends of the earth. He will not grow tired or weary, and his understanding no one can fathom.

A Prayer for God to Use Me...

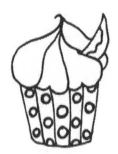

Bible Time

Date:_____

Bible Passage:_____

A Prayer for God's Will...

A Prayer for Faith

What is on Your Mind?

Draw or write about all the things that have been on your mind lately.
Writing down your thoughts can help you to clear your mind.
Focus on your true priorities and pray for each thought.

"If you want something you never had, you have to do
something you have never done."

Give God Your Fears

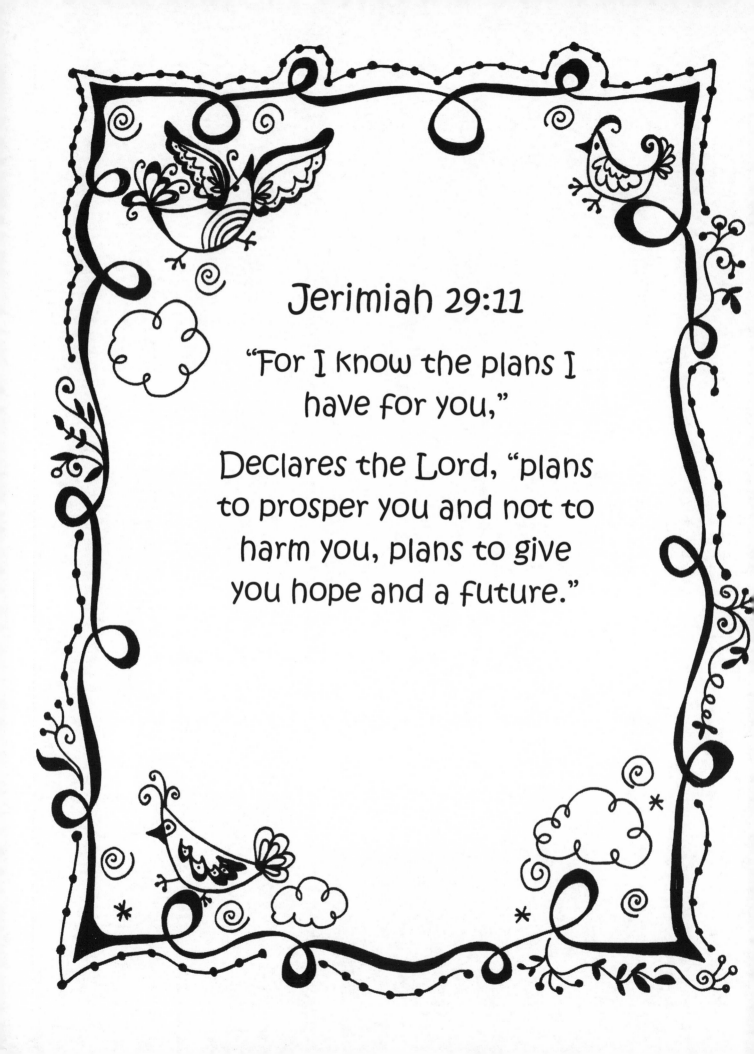

Jerimiah 29:11

"For I know the plans I
have for you,"

Declares the Lord, "plans
to prosper you and not to
harm you, plans to give
you hope and a future."

A Prayer for Family..

Bible Time

Date:_____

Bible Passage:_____

Write a Story

A Prayer for Wisdom

My Thoughts

Draw or write about all the things that have been on your mind lately.
Writing down your thoughts can help you to clear your mind.
Focus on your true priorities and pray for each thought.

Draw Your Dreams...

A Prayer to be Humble...

Bible Time

Date:_____

Bible Passage:_____

I am Thankful For...

A Letter to God

What Is Love?
I loved you. I love you.

I was in the garden of Gethsemane, I knew what was coming,
I wanted to run, but I remembered you.

My child. My child I would do absolutely anything for.
I know you messed up, but that does not stop me from loving
you. Nothing could stop me from loving you.
But you would have to be punished. You would be separated
from me forever.

This was the only way to save you.
My child, my precious child.
The guards came and took me. I didn't fight back.
If this was the only way to save you, I would do anything.

They whipped me, They stabbed me, they spit on me and they
put nails though my hands and feet. I knew this would be
worth it and you would be free. My child wouldn't have to be
condemned. They crushed a crown of thorns on my head, I saw
your face, you would be free. I hung there in excruciating pain
with your guilt on my shoulders. My Father couldn't even look
at me. He turned away. I took one last breath, "IT IS
FINISHED!" you were no longer a slave of the devil.

You were freed. I did this. Even though I knew I would run to
you with open arms and you would turn away and say "I don't
know you." I still did this for you.

Thinking Tree
JOURNALS

Copyright Information

This Journal, and electronic printable downloads are for Home and Family use only. You may make copies of these materials for only the children in your household.

All other uses of this material must be permitted in writing by the Thinking Tree LLC. It is a violation of copyright law to distribute the electronic files or make copies for your friends, associates or students without our permission.

For information on using these materials for businesses, co-ops, summer camps, day camps, daycare, afterschool program, churches, or schools please contact us for licensing.

Contact Us:
The Thinking Tree LLC
617 N. Swope St. Greenfield, IN 46140. United States
317.622.8852 PHONE (Dial +1 outside of the USA) 267.712.7889 FAX
FunSchoolingBooks.com
jbrown@DyslexiaGames.com

Made in the USA
Charleston, SC
19 May 2016